# Tips for Helping Your Aging Parents

## (without losing your mind)

### Kira Reginato

Edited by: Ron Scudder and Valerie Andrews
CreateSpace Independent Publishing Platform, North Charleston, SC
Book Layout ©2013 BookDesignTemplates.com


ISBN: 1530441110

ISBN 13:978-1530441112

Library of Congress Control Number: 2016904032

৩৪

Dedicated to my mom,
a marvelous example of kindness and integrity in this world

# MANY THANKS

To all of my clients and their wonderful family members, who taught me so much of what I'm sharing in this book.

My walk-and-talk-and-process pals: Marian O'Dowd, Cathy Maley, and Cheryl White

My Castle Pad Supporters: Sarah Scudder, motivator extraordinaire; Will Mitchell and Rebecca Gary

My editors at the start: Karuna Gerstein, Paul Markovich, Maria Larsen, Hannah Onstad, Brad Wiley II, Vanessa Bauch, Martha O'Hayer, and Julie Ann Soukoulis

My editors at the end: Valerie Andrews and Ron Scudder, enthusiastically helped me retain my voice throughout the book. Ron, thanks for reminding me to keep it personal. Elaina Hirakida for painstakingly formatting the book and cover with me. Rachel Gordon for the eagle-eyed Lowell proofing of the proof.

Angela Perelli: creator of the final title; I'm so grateful for that! Helped me write and rewrite and continue to take turtle steps to finish.

The Willits Poker Clan: Mike and Shirley Timberman, and Pete and Andrea Onstad for supporting Dad and me all these years.

My float-ideas-by crew: Milena Reginato, Carol Nelson, Rebecca Robbins, Regan Brown, and Bob Cheal

My head cheerleaders: my aunts and the Nelsons, who always send the perfect cards and encouragement. Special thanks to Aunt Linda for believing in me and for investing the first $500 in my company.

Diane Judd: got me organized and professionally polished for my radio show, paving the way for this book.

David Comfort: helps me hold the personal branding and multi-media vision. We're seeing it unfold!

Abigail Huller, photographer: Made me look so good.

Francis Yanak: shared his granddaughter's book so I could be inspired by a great format.

Michael Young: suggested a title, which I still love: Confessions of a Geriatric Care Manager.

My dad, Charles Nelson: let me practice my professional skills on him although I failed sometimes... loved me and was proud of me.

My grandma, Isabel Nelson: showed me how wonderful "old folks" could be; so much so, that I made them my career. Doted on me during every visit to Los Gatos.

Thanks to colleagues who have answered my queries in person and on the radio shows about so many topics, especially Charles E. Symes, II on home care issues.

Staff at the San Francisco Veterans Affairs Medical Center: made my dad so comfortable. In his words, "they made me feel I was their only patient."

Dr. Gerald Hsu: went the extra mile to explain things to both of us, advocated for Dad, remained so positive, got Dad a hospice bed, and visited Dad. I will carry this loving attention in my heart forever.

# Table of Contents

RESOURCES

# You Can Do This!

Are you caring for an aging parent, handling one thing after another, surviving one crisis, and then the next?

Or…

Are you in a calm time, wondering how to prepare for the time when your parent starts slowing down?

Either way, this book is for you.

You may be helping your parents and notice it can be challenging. Our relationship with our parents can be crazy-making. Being consumed with our own lives, the addition of helping manage parents can send us 'round the bend, even though we love them.

I think elder care today is an exhausting, emotionally taxing adventure, sprinkled with some life-changing loving moments and funny spells, too. This is lonely work; often it's just one of us doing most of the assisting. Decades ago we would have had many relatives close by to help. Unfortunately, our elder care system is segmented, often not providing the support the whole family needs.

Clients tell me they wish they had received professional help at the beginning because it would have spared them making errors. This book should help you minimize the common mistakes people make with their time, money, and energy when caring for a loved one.

This book is purposefully short, with easy-to-read sentences. I respect how busy you are and know that the role of caregiver is *on top* of everything else you are doing. I cared for my father for a couple of years so I'm sharing personal tips, as well as professional.

My secret plan is for you to be able to avoid crumbling under the role of caregiving. Caregiving can take a toll on your health and sanity and even on your finances. You probably know the health and sanity effects, but the financial effects of taking time off work to take care of a parent can be very costly. If using the tips in my book make you healthier and wealthier when *you* age, then let's celebrate!

With a hug of support,

Kira Reginato
Petaluma, California

# CHAPTER 1

# Getting Started

Ground rules to keep in mind as you read this book:

1) Help your parent in a gentle way, and be patient with yourself and your siblings. This can be a long journey. No one gets it all right, so be easy on yourself.

2) Keep in mind that you can't expect change from just one talk. Keep the dialogue going. Alternate the hard stuff and the easy stuff, so you don't overwhelm your parent or the others involved in caretaking. We don't want people to dread seeing you because you keep bringing up problems they don't want to face yet. Sometimes you have to let something drop until a window opens and allows renewed discussion.

3) Let yourself be helped. You don't have to go it alone.

4) In my book, I refer to Mom or Dad—but the advice applies to them both and any older adult you may be helping. I know it's not grammatically correct, but to avoid the s/he nomenclature, I refer to Mom and Dad as "they" sometimes.

5) You can do this—with the help of all the preparation hints and guidance in this book. If you're preparing for the future, read the

whole book and get your ducks lined up, chapter by chapter. If you're already a caregiver, check the table of contents, pick out the topic that speaks to where you are, and start there.

# THE FOUR STEPS

## 1. START A MASTER FILE ON YOUR COMPUTER

When your parents are about seventy years old, start a file on your computer for them. Keep a diary of conversations. I called my file "DAD NOTES."

Make entries about any health issues they mention to you - high blood pressure, dizziness, toothache.

Take notes on conversations about events coming up or needs they have. Think about a timeframe to address them - driver's license renewal coming up, trust document to revise, cataract-surgery transportation needed.

Document any incidents or changes in their health and overall status - shortness of breath going up stairs, weight loss, infection.

Having notes to review allows you to look back and see patterns - falls, times in hospital, upset stomach, pneumonia. You can see the timeline when changes began. You can share this information with medical staff, if needed.

Here are sample entries from my file when I was caring for my father:

DAD NOTES: *11/9/11  Dad went to VA. Blood work (fasting) showed elevated PSA, almost double, 2-4 now. VA to call him to go to SF appt. for more work, Needs records from 2004 surgery.*
*Eustachian tube blocked, needs to see ENT specialist in SF.*
*Got flu and tetanus shots.*
*12/16/14  Took Dad to beach. When I go to get him in apartment, he is wheezing, hard for him to dress, undies on inside out, suspenders backward. He refuses to let me turn them around, says they are on right.*

## 2. COMPILE A LIST OF MEDICATIONS

According to the Centers for Disease Control, "As people age, they typically take more medicines. Older adults (sixty-five years or older) are twice as likely as others to come to emergency rooms for adverse drug events (over 177,000 emergency visits each year), and nearly seven times more likely to be hospitalized after an emergency visit."

You want to understand the medications your parent is taking and to make sure they are taken as prescribed.

**Ask Dad if you can sit down with him and make a list of all current medications, vitamins, and supplements.** (See template provided)

In my experience, people rarely keep meds and supplements in one place. Be persistent, and be sure to search the house. The medications might be in a kitchen drawer, a bedside table, or the bathroom.

This exercise will give you an appreciation for the number of prescriptions he takes and whether he knows why he's taking each med.

DAD NOTES: *My dad only took one medication for years: Lisinopril. When I asked him why he took it, he had no idea. When I asked, "Could it be for high blood pressure?" he would say, "Oh, no, I don't have high blood pressure." When I checked with his doctor, he verified that Dad had high blood pressure.*

I noticed that the sicker my dad became and the more meds he was prescribed, the harder it was for him to understand what he was taking or why. This is common.

## MEDICATION LIST

Allergies to medication and the reaction:

_____

_____

Pharmacy:

_____

Address: _____

Phone: _____

| Medication or Supplement Name | Dose | When taking? | Why taking? |
|---|---|---|---|
| Example: Lisinopril | 10 mg | AM | High blood pressure |
| | | | |
| | | | |
| | | | |
| | | | |
| | | | |
| | | | |
| | | | |

| Medication or Supplement Name | Dose | When taking? | Why taking? |
|---|---|---|---|
| | | | |
| | | | |
| | | | |
| | | | |
| | | | |
| | | | |

BONUS: A discussion about medications gently opens the door to talk about your loved one's health problems.

Enter the completed medication list in your computer file, and keep a hard copy for the Communication Binder you'll be making later in Chapter 3.

If you find expired or unused meds, see if Dad agrees to remove them from the house. If he insists on keeping them, put the old meds in a separate place where he won't take them by mistake.

Expired meds are toxic waste, so you can't just throw them in the garbage. The dump, pharmacy, or hospital may accept them.

**Purchase a pill box.**

Pill boxes can be purchased at pharmacies or from
HealthAccessories.com or MedMinder.com. Search under "Pill
boxes."

Models vary depending on how many times meds are taken per
day. A pill box accommodates meds taken from one to four times
a day, with a separate slot for each time frame such as morning,
noon, evening, and bedtime.

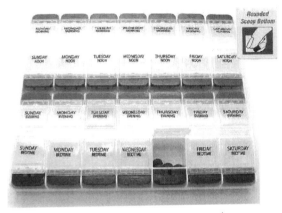

*(Photo courtesy of www.healthaccessories.com)*

**If your parent is agreeable, fill the medication container
together.**

Please don't let your loved one take medication willy-nilly from
bottles left at bedside, in the bathroom, or on the kitchen counter.
Organization of meds is very important. Even if it's one pill a day,
put it into the pill box. Put in vitamins and all of the necessary
over-the-counter meds. The earlier you and your parent get in the

habit of using this system to reduce errors that can lead to hospital stays, the better.

Develop a routine of filling the medication container weekly. Or, fill additional containers and put aside, ready to go.

DAD NOTES: *Initially, my dad refused to use a pill box, saying he could remember what to take when. After one hospital stay, however, when it was evident he was not taking meds as prescribed, I insisted. Once he used the box, he loved it and told me he had no idea how he could have managed without it. He told me repeatedly how happy he was to have my help managing his meds.*

Take the team approach: fill the compartments with the medication for each day while your parent watches, or they can fill the container and you can watch. Two sets of eyes help prevent errors, such as missing or doubling up on a dose.

It's best to keep all the medication bottles in one place, so that when it comes time to fill the pill box, you have everything you need. It's also easier to check what meds need refills; you don't want to risk running out.

**If medications and supplements are consistent,** ask your pharmacist about a customized drug packaging system, such as medi-strip or blister pack.

Medi-strips organize medications by time of day and date. All pills (even vitamins) are packed in individually labeled disposable strips.

It's easy to take the right medication at the right time, simply pull and tear the pouch for that time of day.

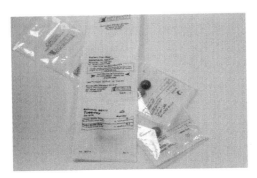

*(Photo courtesy of Golden Gate Pharmacy)*

Blister packs are similar; they contain the medication for a specific time of day also.

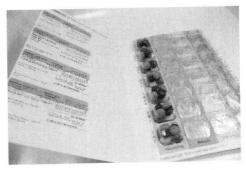

*(Photo courtesy of Golden Gate Pharmacy)*

With either of these individualized packaging systems, there are no bottles to handle, no pill box is needed, and the systems are delivered to the home.

There are high-tech solutions for medication management such as dispensing machines like the one sold by Philips at www.ManageMyPills.com.

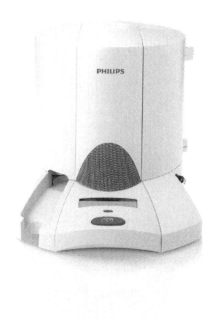

*(Photo courtesy of Philips Healthcare, Philips Lifeline)*

## 3. GET A STATE ID FROM DMV

This is especially helpful if your parent's driver's license has expired. Having a valid state ID allows your parent to sign legal documents, such as a trust or power of attorney.

## 4. FOR FUN, MAKE A MUSIC PLAYLIST

Add all your parent's favorite songs, along with a few good podcasts, too, on topics that catch their interest. Grandkids usually love to help with this task, and it can be a wonderful way to connect them with the grandparents.

Store this list on their phone and yours, so you have it handy in the future. They can play the music and podcasts when in the hospital or emergency room. Nothing beats music to keep you entertained while you wait.

# CHAPTER 2

# Check Home Safety

Here's a scary statistic:

**"Falls are the leading cause of fatal and non-fatal injuries for older Americans."** (National Council on Aging)

You may not be able to prevent your loved one's every fall, but spending the time to reduce risk may be worth it to avoid an emergency room visit, a hospital stay, a rehab stay, and even death. Remember, you may have to be in charge of that journey. Save yourself the trouble by reducing falling risks now.

FACTS ABOUT FALLING from Learnnottofall.com

- About one third of those over 65 fall each year, and the risk increases with age.
- Those who fall are two to three times more likely to fall again.
- 47% of people who fall and aren't injured cannot get up without assistance.
- Falls account for 25% of all hospital admissions, and 40% of all nursing home admissions.
- The period of time elders who fall spend immobile often affects their health outcome. Muscle cell breakdown starts

to occur within 30–60 minutes of compression due to falling. Dehydration, pressure sores, hypothermia, and pneumonia may result.

- 40% of those admitted to the hospital do not return to independent living; 25% die within a year.

Your job: Conduct a twenty-three question household-safety assessment.

I use this tool with clients and invite you to use my form. This form is not exhaustive but addresses some basics for reducing falls and accidents.

While you are at it, look at your own home and reduce your risks. It's never too early.

TIP: Do the household-safety assessment in two parts. Don't try to fix each problem as you take inventory, or you will become sidetracked.

I provide ideas for addressing problems at the end of this chapter.

## PART 1

Walk through the home, filling out the form as you go.

### HOUSEHOLD-SAFETY CHECKLIST

Yes/No          Pathways and hallways clear?

Y/N    Walker or wheelchair fits through doorways and pathways easily?

Y/N    Handrails on stairs inside home securely attached?

Y/N    Adequate lighting in each room in daytime?

Y/N    Adequate lighting at night?

Y/N    Night-lights needed?

Y/N    Grab bars in shower?

Y/N    Skid strips or textured mat on floor of shower/bathtub?

Y/N    Grab bars by toilet?

Y/N    Carpets in good repair? Note: Worn areas produce uneven surfaces, which cause falls.

Y/N    Throw rugs attached securely so they don't slip around?

Y/N    Cords or wires exposed that could cause tripping?

Y/N    Can your parent easily care for pets without bending over?

Y/N    Smoke detectors on each level of home working?

Y/N    Fire extinguisher location known, nearby, and charged?

Y/N    Is cooking area safe, with no flammable items near the burners?

Y/N    Is there a telephone landline in case of emergency and if cell phones don't work?

Y/N    Phone next to bed, in case of emergency?

Y/N    Is phone easy to dial, with oversized numbers and back lighting?

Y/N    Weapons in home? If so, are they loaded or unloaded?

Y/N    Door locks working?

Y/N    Secure handrails on stairs outside home?

Y/N    Does parent have a personal emergency response system in case of emergency/accident?

# PART 2

Review the form and think about where to make safety improvements. The sooner you do these, the better. Please don't wait until *after* the fall!

DAD NOTES: *My dad parked his TV in the middle of his living room and ran the cord across the carpet, right in front of the kitchen. He told me the TV had to be there so he could have his sofa bed pulled out and the TV at his feet. If it had been against the wall, I guess he couldn't see or hear it too well. Drove me crazy with worry. I bought a mat and taped it down over the cord, so he and I wouldn't trip. It was not pretty, but he never fell, so it worked.*

## WHO DOES WHAT?

Nonworking items, such as a fire extinguisher, a smoke alarm, or a burned-out light are easy fixes. So is picking up items from the floor so no one trips. Other fixes require a licensed contractor. Jump on all the easy stuff you can do, and make a list for the contractor to do. Then set up an appointment to have those items addressed.

Some cities have programs that assist with home repairs, small and large. Call Eldercare Locator (800) 677-1116; to find out more, go to Eldercare.gov.

## SOLUTIONS TO REDUCE FALL AND ACCIDENT RISK

- If a walker or a wheelchair does not fit through a doorway, ask the contractor to rehang the door so there is more room. You can make it swing in the opposite direction, or remove it all together.

- Install railings on *both* sides of the steps.

- Put in brighter light bulbs where needed.

- Install night-lights. I suggest doing so near the *bottom* of a wall to illuminate paths when walking, especially from bed to bathroom. I like motion-sensor lights because they are not on all night. I give my clients Light Angels from www.asseenontv.com.

- Make it easier to care for pets: place the cat litter box on a higher surface so there's no bending over to clean it.

- Hire a dog walker, especially if the weather is cold, hot, or wet.

- Consider if you want to discuss removing weapons from the house. Elderly males, in particular, may use them for suicide, and removing them may be a good proactive measure.

*(Photo courtesy of Kerr Medical DME Inc.)*

- If a parent needs supervision getting in and out of bed, consider a wireless floor mat that signals an alarm in another room so you can be alerted to assist. Order from KerrMedical.com. Prices vary depending on size and type you purchase.

- Throw rugs may seem innocent, but they are not. Those suckers slip and slide, and people go flying, so, try to do one of the following:

Get permission to toss the throw rugs. This is best. I regularly remove them during my first visit, even if people think this is high-handed of me. They are *that* dangerous.

Put double-sided tape around the perimeters of the throw rugs so that they stay in place, or get new ones with better rubber backing. Cost of new rug: $40. Cost of new hip: thousands.

For carpet runners and rugs with fringe, try to get permission to roll them up and store them.

- Have grab bars installed inside and outside shower area.

- Have grab bars installed next to toilet area. You would be surprised how many people use the towel rack for this and rip it out of the wall.

- To avoid tripping accidents, remove clutter. Pay close attention to items on closet floors.

- Repair broken or uneven steps inside and outside the home.

- Do chores that require a ladder.

If you can persuade your parent not to get up on the step stool because *you* offer to do the ladder-type chores, go for it, if you feel comfortable.

- Put contrasting color tape on the edge of stairs inside the home so they are well delineated from each other. It may prevent a broken bone.

- Paint the outside step edges with a contrasting color to assist with depth perception decline. We just painted three short strips of white paint on one particular step, which people tended to miss on our walkway. Now they notice that step.

- Call California Telephone Access Program to get a free phone with big buttons or other features that help with diminished sight, hearing, or cognition (800) 806-1191. If you live outside of California, they will provide the program information for your area.

## "WHILE YOU ARE AT IT" IDEAS

- Purchase a waterproof mattress cover for the bed.

- If getting up and down from the couch is difficult, buy Assist-A-Tray. Manufactured by Stander Products, available from Parentgiving.com.

*(Photo courtesy of Stander Products)*

- If getting in and out of bed or turning in bed is challenging, purchase under-the-mattress grab bars or a Bed Cane. Manufactured by Stander Products, available from Parentgiving.com, EZ Adjust Bed Rail or Bed Cane.

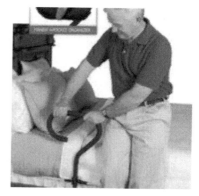

*(Photos courtesy of Stander Products)*

- If getting in and out of a garage due to stairs is an issue, consider a ramp.

- If getting in and out of the car is an issue, buy a Swivel Seat Cushion, like a lazy Susan for your bottom. Also consider a Handibar, that you can lean on. Manufactured by Stander Products, available from Parentgiving.com.

*(Photos courtesy of Stander Products)*

- Consider getting your parent a Personal Emergency Response System (PERS).

If your mom falls in her house, how soon would someone find her? Many older adults live alone, so when they fall it can be hours, or even days, before someone discovers them. It's really sad when clients tell me about their falls, how long they were on the ground, the pain they were in, how cold they were, and how afraid and helpless they felt.

If clients are refusing PERS, I gently point out that a family member would find me quickly if I fell. I ask, "Is that true for you?" Once they ponder that question, they usually agree to try a PERS (and their children get peace of mind).

I usually recommend the brand Lifeline for a PERS, but there are many companies. Lifeline offers two services: Basic or Auto Alert.

BASIC: Your Mom can put a pendant around her neck or wear it like a watch. Whenever she presses the button, she is connected to the Lifeline Response Center for immediate assistance.

Buttons are waterproof, so can be worn bathing, although many people take it off before bathing and then regret it because so many falls happen in the bathroom.

*(Photo courtesy of Philips Healthcare, Philips Lifeline)*

AUTO ALERT: This also has a pendant, but with Auto Alert function, one doesn't have to push the button. The pendant senses when the wearer has fallen and immediately sends help. This option is recommended for people with memory loss, who may forget to push the button, or for people who are reluctant, for whatever reason, to summon help.

For about fifty dollars a month (in my area), this is money well spent. You can push the call button if fearful of an intruder, too. See www.LIFELINESYS.com, (800) 949-2434.

### DO THE HOUSEHOLD-SAFETY ASSESSMENT TODAY!

You can do this. Once you reduce some of the risks, you'll rest easier. Making the attempt may alleviate some of your guilt if Mom or Dad does end up falling. Life is not perfect and there will always be risks. Being proactive will minimize accidents.

**One extra thought:** Alcohol, medications, and over-the-counter meds can cause falls. Seemingly innocent medication, such as Advil PM and Benadryl, should be avoided in older adults. If you are concerned about this, think about harm-reduction techniques, as well as addressing addiction issues.

Misuse of alcohol and drugs usually causes *more* issues as we age, and it doesn't resolve itself without help. If it's time to suggest professional treatment, consider speaking to a care manager or therapist about bringing up this important topic.

Check out these two resources for more info about medications and older adults:

**Beers Criteria:**
http://www.americangeriatrics.org/files/documents/beers/Beers CriteriaPublicTranslation.pdf

**START STOPP List**
http://www.ngna.org/_resources/documentation/chapter/carolin a_mountain/STARTandSTOPP.pdf

# CHAPTER 3

# Prepare a Grab-and-Go Bag

To ensure maximum readiness for hospital or emergency room visits, create a Grab-and-Go Bag as soon as possible. I ask clients to make these up.

## A GRAB-AND-GO BAG CONSISTS OF TWO PARTS:

1) A Hospital Visit Binder, filled with vital information a medical professional may need at the hospital

2) Personal Items

NOTE: In Chapter 4, you make another binder for *you* to keep and add to over the years. Much of the information will be the same.

Allow two hours to create and assemble items for the binder and another thirty minutes to gather personal items into a backpack or suitcase.

**To make a Hospital Visit Binder, you will need:**

- Three-ring binder and paper
- Ten to fifteen dividers
- Three-hole punch

- Package of five plastic sheets that hold standard 8½ × 11" pages
- Plastic sheets designed to hold business cards, called Business Card Pages, available online or at office supply stores, as below

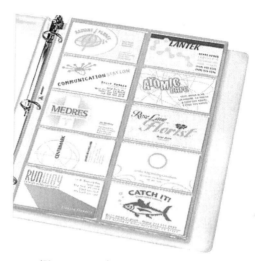

*(Photo courtesy of Avery Products Corporation)*

## PART ONE—HOW TO ASSEMBLE
## HOSPITAL VISIT BINDER

IF your parent has a POLST (Physicians Orders for Life-Sustaining Treatment) form or a DNR (Do Not Resuscitate) form, then steps one or two apply. If they don't have these forms, skip to step three.

1) Place a *copy* of the hot-pink POLST at the front of the binder. The original may be posted already on the refrigerator. Leave the

original form on the refrigerator, where emergency help will see it.

2) Place a *copy* of the DNR form at the front of the binder. The original may be posted already on the refrigerator. Leave the original form on the refrigerator, where emergency help will see it.

You may wish to take a picture of these forms with your phone so you have mobile access to the data at any time.

3) Create a cover sheet for front of binder that says:

Info for Hospital

Patient:_____

4) Label a divider PATIENT INFO

Prepare a sheet in your computer, such as the example provided on next page, with your loved one's information.

Keeping it in your computer allows for easy updates. Email it to yourself so you have access from a mobile device.

Put completed form in binder.

**PATIENT NAME:**                    Date of Birth:
Address:
Cell Phone:                          Home Phone:


Health Insurance info:


Medical Record #:
Medicare #:
Social Security #:


Veterans #:


Primary care doctor:
Address:
Phone:                               Fax:


**EMERGENCY CONTACTS:**
(Note if anyone is legal agent for making health-care decisions)


Name/Relationship:                   Cell:
Work:


Name/Relationship:                   Cell:
Work:


Long-Term Care Insurance Company:
Policy ID Number:
Address:
Phone:                               Fax:

Long-term care insurance covers:
      Home Care (Nonmedical)? _____
      Assisted Living? _____
      Skilled Nursing Care? _____

Maximum amount paid per month by long-term care insurance:
$_____

⅋⅋

5) Label a divider HEALTH INSURANCE

Make a copy of all health insurance cards, both front and back. Put these copies in a plastic sheet and place in binder.

6) Label the next divider MEDICATION

Insert a copy of the medication list you've already made in Chapter 1. See, all your hard work is paying off already.

7) Label a divider DIAGNOSES

Create a list of your parent's health issues. What is the easiest way to do this? Ask your parent's doctor to print out this information to go in this binder.

*Example of Diagnoses list:*

High blood pressure
Congestive heart failure
Depression
Diabetes

8) Label a divider LEGAL

Insert a copy of the completed power of attorney for health care document and/or the advance health care directive form. These documents give you, or the designated agent, the right to make medical decisions for your parent, if he/she is incapable. Hospital staff may want to see a copy of this document.

9) Insert blank sheets of paper. You can use these to take notes when you are at the doctor's office, or at the hospital or emergency room.

## PART TWO—PACKING PERSONAL ITEMS

Find a backpack or suitcase to hold the Hospital Visit Binder, and then add these essentials:

- Robe
- Change of clothes and pair of shoes to wear home
- Spare eyeglasses
- Hairbrush, comb, toothbrush, toothpaste
- Book/magazine
- Note pad and pen
- Change for vending machines (My dad wanted the newspaper and candy)
- Earbuds for electronic device/phone to listen to music and podcasts
- Extra phone charger, if needed
- Mirror, makeup, if desired

Congratulations, the Grab-and-Go Bag is now complete. When the time comes to take your parent for medical treatment, you will feel prepared and more confident. The medical staff will be very appreciative of this helpful information at their fingertips.

Decide where to put the Grab-and-Go Bag. Tell all family and caregivers where they can find the bag, to be given to the emergency medical staff when they arrive or for you to grab before heading to the hospital.

Put a note on the refrigerator for the EMTs, giving the location of the Grab-and-Go Bag/medical information. EMTs are trained to look on the fridge for any medical forms, but they need to know about this vital bag.

# CHAPTER 4

# Communication Binder: For Your Reference

Personally, I must have referred to the binder I made of Dad's information a hundred times in the two years before he died, and even after he died. Having his information in my computer and in the binder made my life a lot easier.

**This Communication Binder is similar to the one you created for the Grab-and-Go Bag. It has additional reference material that a hospital won't need, but you will.**

1) For this binder, make dividers and a copy of all you included in the Hospital Visit Binder for the Grab-and-Go Bag: patient information sheet, diagnoses list, medication list, legal information, and health insurance cards.

2) For easy reference, place a plastic sheet that holds business cards in front of your binder. Insert all business cards you have for professionals your loved one is working with.

3) Label a divider tab for each doctor your parent sees, noting the doctor's name or area of practice. Example: Dr. Tsu, Dr. Roman,

etc., or Primary Doctor, Cardiologist. Place any documents you have from their offices into the binder for reference.

4) If applicable, make a copy of DD-214 Veterans' paperwork and insert it into the binder. I put my dad's in a plastic sheet, so he or I could find it easily.

5) Label a divider LONG-TERM CARE INSURANCE and place a copy of the policy here. You may need to refer to this over the years to read the fine print.

6) Label a divider HOSPITAL PAPERS. Insert copies of lab results, medication instructions, discharge summaries, etc.

7) There are private papers that don't go in your parent's Grab-and-Go Bag, but you'll want to take the time to gather them and make sure they are up-to-date. Keep them in your binder under LEGAL, if possible:

- Power of attorney for finances
- Trust documents
- Will

Tell at least one other family member where he or she can find these documents if they are not included in your binder.

8) Read over and insert a copy of the following checklist to prepare for a hospital stay.

## CONSIDER COMPLETING BEFORE A HOSPITAL STAY:

☐ Give a trusted person a spare key to my home.

☐ Choose a home care agency or caregiver to hire, if needed, when I come home.

☐ Have cash on hand to provide to someone who can buy groceries or meds or needed equipment for me.

☐ Buy extra hearing aid batteries.

☐ Ask someone to be my hospital advocate, available to speak and listen to what the hospital staff says.

☐ Decide how I want visitors handled.

☐ Complete my durable power of attorney for health care form; explain my health-care wishes to my agent.

## WHILE IN HOSPITAL, ARRANGE FOR SOMEONE TO DO THE FOLLOWING:

☐ Pay bills.

☐ Water houseplants (and garden).

☐ Take care of pets.

☐ Bring in mail and newspapers.

☐ Notify people I am in the hospital; make a list of whom *not* to call.

☐ Check e-mail.

☐ Check phone messages.

## IF LEFT HOME BY AMBULANCE, ARRANGE FOR SOMEONE TO:

☐ Care for pets.

☐ Put out trash; empty house garbage.

☐ Clean out refrigerator.

☐ Return rented movies and library books.

☐ Wash dishes.

☐ Tidy house.

## PRIOR TO LEAVING HOSPITAL, ARRANGE FOR SOMEONE TO DO THE FOLLOWING:

☐ Shop for food.

☐ Make some meals.

☐ Change bed linens.

☐ Tidy house.

☐ Fill all the prescriptions from hospital in advance so I have medication *in hand* when I leave hospital.

☐ Decide what help will be needed to handle stairs at my home.

☐ Ask for someone to purchase any durable medical equipment (shower chair, transfer bench, raised toilet seat, etc.) I may need.

☐ Arrange for person to transport me home.

☐     Arrange for someone to stay with me first night or so.

☐     Decide if I want visitors at home and how soon; ask one person to explain situation to friends for me, if needed.

☐     Ask clergy to visit, if desired.

☐     Ask someone to make hair/nail care appointment for me (to come to my home, if needed).

"Living Ideas for Elders," compiled by Kira Reginato, on behalf of American Society on Aging conference members, September, 2009

# CHAPTER 5

# Legally Honoring Your Parent's Health Wishes

Fill out one of these forms:

Power of Attorney for Health Care

OR

Advance Health Care Directive

## PURPOSE

All of us over eighteen years old need to complete one of the above forms in case we get to a point where we can't speak for ourselves. It's not about finances; this one is just for medical decisions.

It's not about giving up control. If you can make every medical decision for yourself until you die, you will. But if you ever need someone at your hospital bedside to make decisions, nominate an agent now and discuss your thoughts with them. These advance conversations are key.

## BE PERSISTENT

It took me two years to get my father to sign his own power of attorney for health care. Many people are superstitious about discussing what could go wrong toward the end of life—thinking and talking about this stuff seems prohibited. Maybe Dad resisted for this reason, but who knows?

DAD NOTES: *I would remind my dad to complete the form and he'd say, "Okay, just leave it there on the table." Then...nothing. I pleaded with him to fill out the darn form and he'd say "You know my wishes." I did, however, I also told him "Medical staff may not listen to me without a document proving to them that I'm your legal agent and therefore allowed to speak on your behalf." Still, he didn't complete the form.*

*So, one day, I just filled out the form, guessing at what he would have wanted. Then I handed the document to him when he was lounging outside, waiting for me to bring him lunch, and said, "Dad, sign this. If you don't, I won't give bring you your sandwich!" He laughed and signed it, and I put it in the binder I kept for him, and that was it.*

## WHERE TO GET A FORM

Hospitals may have these forms and there are many on the internet. Some examples online are: Caringinfo.org, AgingwithDignity.org (5 Wishes form is $5.00), or NHDD.org.

## COMPLETING A FORM

Rest assured that forms come with instructions on how to complete them.

Some towns offer a workshop on completing a power of attorney for health care form. In our town, our hospice company, among others, leads the workshop.

> To make things fun, I threw a party and invited friends and family over; I gave the forms to everyone, and we watched a short video put out by AgingwithDignity.org, using form called Five Wishes.
>
> We had homemade lasagna, garlic bread, salad, wine, and cake. We laughed and had a fun time discussing how to approach this, what to fill out, and so forth. Feel free to do the same.

The best approach I've found for completing the form is to sit down with your parent and fill it out *with him/her.*

While you are thinking about this issue, I suggest that you fill out your own form and nominate an agent for yourself. Filling out the forms together opens up rich conversation about values and fears, as you discuss some difficult scenarios. It can bring a closeness and tenderness you didn't expect.

1) You should each consider two people you trust who could represent and honor your wishes. List one as your primary person and one as backup. They are called your "agents."

When you are considering whom to name, keep in mind that it may be wise to appoint nonfamily members. The nonfamily member may be less emotional and more pragmatic if decisions need to be made. I asked my mom if she would be my primary agent, and she said she would prefer not to do so. She said that it would be hard on her since I'm her daughter; I hadn't considered that. I chose a nurse friend to be my primary agent and Mom as my backup agent instead.

2) CRITICAL: Have a conversation with your two agents about the medical interventions you might or might not want, in case you can't speak for yourself after some health event.

Have the agents take notes to remember the conversation or make a short video so you have an accurate reminder of what your parent said. You/Agents can watch it later, if there are doubts or questions about what was said.

I had a client who wanted CPR, even though the doctor explained that her outcome would be poor, with possible broken ribs and possible brain damage. She insisted on receiving CPR if her heart stopped, and that's what we wrote on her form. Luckily she passed in her sleep on hospice, so no CPR was ever needed.

## <u>ONCE DONE</u>

1) Once the form is completed, give a copy to your parent's doctor, for the chart.

2) If you completed a form for yourself, give this to your doctor for your chart.

3) Provide a copy to the medical records department at your local hospital.

4) Put a copy in both of the Communication Binders you made.

---

REMEMBER: If you wait too long, your parent, or you, may lose the ability to sign the document legally, due to mental changes such as dementia.

You want to complete a form and have conversations well in advance and as health changes come up.

---

# CHAPTER 6

# Accompany Your Parent to a Doctor's Appointment

This is a good way to establish a line of communication with Mom or Dad's medical team.

You want to form a rapport with physicians *before* issues become serious. You may be the one calling to check on lab results or medication refills when your parent isn't up to it. When you attend an appointment, the physician sees you as a source of support and information. This physician is more likely to chat with you by phone when a crisis arises. You want this connection—and so does the doctor.

This relationship can be even more vital when you are dealing with a loved one who has memory issues.

## THE FIRST DOCTOR VISIT

1) Bring a copy of the advance health care directive with you.

2) If there is confidential information about Mom that the physician needs ahead of time (a particular concern you wish to address), you may hand it to the receptionist when you arrive or fax the information ahead of time. If possible, send it via e-mail.

You are free to tell the doctor your concerns; he or she would just need authorization from the patient before responding to questions.

3) During the first doctor visit with your parent, I recommend being a quiet observer. If you dominate, you may appear disrespectful or overbearing. Instead, observe the interaction between Mom and the doctor.

4) Offer to excuse yourself at some point so Mom and the physician can interact privately.

5) Ask the doctor for a list of diagnoses, and put a copy in both Communication Binders. This list will be of great value if your parent goes to the emergency room.

Take notes at the doctor's appointment to review with your parent later. It's easy to miss instructions or fail to absorb all that the doctor covers.

DAD NOTES: *1/30/13—We went to Dr. Hsu (oncologist). Notes from appt.: Watching for low blood count, as this is sign of lymph worsening. Does not see any indication of this, so no reason to think lymph aggressive.*
*Spot under arm now palpable, was not before. About two fingers in width. Labs look good now; doctor wants LDH measured today (we went to lab for draw; low before—78 now). Good news. LDH is enzyme in cells; when tumors are active, they break apart. We might see high numbers if lymphoma worsening. If node gets bigger, we can decide then to take out node in general surgery; he'd do bone-marrow biopsy at hips (local, not general anesthetic).*

*If no fever, weight loss, chills, drenching sheets, good energy level—no worries.*

*BP 125/68 today, vitals great. Dad told doctor of pain at incision site few weeks ago, probably stretched where scar was, muscle. Not to worry. If feels warm, take temperature; 5 percent body weight loss in six months is a concern.*

*Renewed Lisinopril for us; hope will mail. Pharmacy ordered more calcium for him, to be delivered.*

Note: I took these notes which may not be accurate, but this is what I understood during the appt.

If you are not able to accompany your mom, ask her if she would sign a release, allowing you to speak with her doctor. There are federal rules requiring written authorization to receive another person's medical information. These are called HIPAA regulations.

A sample authorization note, seen on next page, can be tailored for your use. Ask your parent to sign and then give to the physician.

If your parent refuses this permission, revisit the issue at another time.

Sample Doctor Letter

Date: _____

To: Dr. _____

This letter gives permission for you to communicate about my health condition with

_____. Thank you.

            Insert name of family member

Sincerely,

_____

            Insert name of patient

# THE SECOND DOCTOR VISIT

Now that you have met the doctor, and he or she understands your role more fully, you may want to ask questions to get a better handle on Mom's health condition. How do you go about this? Each loved one is different.

Option 1) If there are specific questions that need answers, share them with your Mom and encourage her to ask the doctor. This will empower her. She is the patient, after all.

Option 2) Some parents appreciate your asking the questions, as it shows your concern. They feel your support and it reinforces your relationship with them. It is an act of love. Others may be too ill or have memory loss and may be unable to track the conversation or ask questions. Make sure you *ask permission from your parent* before you speak directly to the doctor, to show respect.

Pack up all of your parent's meds and supplements to take to this visit, or bring the medication list you made earlier.

Ask the doctor if Mom can eliminate any meds.   This is considered part of a medication review. This can save money as well as time getting medications refilled, and it will eliminate any unnecessary medications. Get permission from Mom before requesting, so she doesn't panic that she might lose her favorite antianxiety medication.

# CHAPTER 7

# Thinking About Yourself and the Future as a Caregiver

## DIFFICULT TERRITORY

I understand you might be hesitant to discuss caregiving issues with your parents, especially if you don't already have a close relationship with them. At this time of life, these conversations are even harder.

Maybe your parents were abusive, neglectful, unhealthy, mentally ill, or just plain unhelpful when you were growing up. Now they want something from us which may be difficult to give.

Time and time again, I have seen adult children act incredibly diligent and loyal, despite the difficult childhood experiences they may have had. Most of the time they want to help and it's the parent who stonewalls.

How do you step in now to take care of people who may not have done a very good job of caring for you?

How do you set heathly boundaries and limits to your time, regardless of how close you are to your parent?

When appropriate, I give clients and their families a questionnaire to complete. This can provide insight into concerns before meeting with them. If you complete one, it allows you a chance to quantify how you might want to help, and what you don't wish to do. Be honest with yourself. There is no sense committing to something you don't want to do. It has the potential to become a burden that brings misery, stress, or resentment.

---

Keep in mind the costs to your health, time, and wallet when caregiving. The June, 2011 MetLife study reported that "**the out-of-pocket costs for caregivers for someone older than fifty years of age averaged $5,531 per year.**"

On a national level, we are spending $3 trillion on caregiving, and pitching in to help Mom or Dad can cost close to $300,000 for us over a lifetime including lost wages, contributions to pensions and Social Security (MetLife Study of Caregiving Costs to Working Caregivers).

---

DAD NOTES: *I would drive eighty miles round trip to take Dad to the VA for appointments in San Francisco. He always insisted we get there way early so we could grab breakfast. By the time we got there early, had breakfast, had the appointment, did his labs, got him lunch, and came home, it might be six to eight hours altogether. Sometimes he would give me twenty dollars for gas and bridge toll and treat me to lunch. I lost hours of wages, but I wanted to be there for him, and he needed me to be there.*

Consider asking your whole family to complete a questionnaire. Perhaps you can have a conversation about the answers, or maybe not.

When older adults fill in the form, it helps articulate emotions, they may not easily share otherwise. Putting thoughts on paper can be easier.

Discussing the answers to what you and your parent write allows you to learn each other's expectations. It's all there in black and white. It's helpful to have these questionnaires completed prior to a hospital stay.

Even if you don't see each other's answers, the pot will have been stirred with food for thought.

## SIBLING RIVALRY

This comes up with elder care a lot. Overbearing siblings and siblings with hidden agendas are common. If you can't handle this added stress, consider making an appointment for a consult with a geriatric care manager (see Chapter 14). Having a professional working with the family to guide the design of a master plan minimizes family conflicts.

If siblings don't want to help or can't, maybe they can *pay* a person to do their part, or maybe *you* want to pay someone to do your part. That's an option if you have the funds.

Check out the RESOURCES section on movie suggestions and books to address sibling rivalry.

There is more info on having a family meeting in Chapter 10.

## SUPPORT-SYSTEM QUESTIONNAIRE

1) How many hours per week would you estimate you spend on caregiving responsibilities (driving, running errands, preparing meals, handling medication, doing hands-on care, etc.)?

_____

2) Are you able and interested in continuing that amount of time on caregiving responsibilities?

_____

If not, what amount of time would be realistic, given your current schedule?

_____

3) What help do you think your loved one could use that s/he isn't receiving?

_____

4) What are you good at or wish to do on behalf of your loved one? For instance, phone work, attending medical appointments, shopping, bill paying, research, etc.

_____

5) What would you prefer to have others/paid help do?

_____

6) Fill in the blank: If only my loved one knew_____

_____


Name_____

Date_____

## PARENT QUESTIONNAIRE

1) How many hours per week would you estimate your caregiver spends on caregiving responsibilities on your behalf (driving, running errands, preparing meals, handling medication, doing hands-on care, calling insurance company, etc.)? _____

2) Do you believe you need less, more, or different help than you are receiving?

_____

3) Is there any type of assistance you would find helpful?

_____

4) If you could change <u>one</u> thing about the current situation, what would it be?

_____

5) Are you aware of any health issues that have surfaced for your caregiver?

_____

6) Has your caregiver been treated for the health issues?

_____

7) What are your plans/goals for the next year?

_____

_____

8) Fill in the blank: If only my loved ones knew_____

_____

Name_____

Date_____

# CHAPTER 8

# Staying Sane in the Emergency Room

## CONSIDERATIONS BEFORE THE EMERGENCY ROOM

Be sure the Grab-and-Go Bag is packed so family or ambulance staff can access it easily and bring to the hospital.

There is typically a long wait in the emergency room. If you want to avoid "waiting in chairs," then you need to call an ambulance. The medical staff will give your parent preferential treatment and attend to him or her sooner. Do consider, however, that Medicare and/or other insurance may not cover the cost of the ambulance ride. You may get stuck with a bill.

Talk with your parent honestly about their health care wishes, if you weren't thorough enough when you created the advance health care directive or power of attorney for health care. What does she *not* want to happen on this visit? The more you clarify *before* Mom or Dad enters the medical system, the better.

## AT THE EMERGENCY ROOM

Bring the Grab-and-Go Bag you already packed. Look at how prepared you are. Good job!

Take this book along so you can read tips while you are there.

If you are Mom's advocate, be prepared to share some of the contents of the Communication Binder with the medical staff. They may take a copy of the advance health care directive, the medication list, the emergency contact list, and the health insurance cards.

Be prepared to give a brief history to the doctor, unless your parent is willing and able. If you have time, you can also print out a few pages of recent history from the computer diary you've been keeping.

> I let clients tell their medical history and only offer to step in or augment their report if it's getting off course or is inaccurate. If you want to politely assist, consider saying, "Mom, do you mind if I tell the doctor about what led us to the emergency room today?"

## HOW TO ADVOCATE AND CARE FOR YOUR PARENT IN THE ER

- If it's been hours since Dad has had food or water, ask staff what his status is and if he can eat or drink. They may offer to send up a tray or bring ice chips. But he may *not* be

allowed to eat or drink if surgery or tests are pending, so
be sure to check. If he can eat, this may be a good time to
leave and get healthy food for both of you to enjoy.

- Ask if you can dim the light so Dad can close his eyes. Rest,
  even for a short time, is important for him—and for you.

- While waiting, get out the music/podcasts and the ear
  buds so your loved one can listen to the playlist you
  created.

- Write down what tests are completed, their results, what
  the doctor tells you, and any questions you can think of,
  while you're waiting. Use the blank binder paper in the
  Communication Binder.

- Ask for other comfort items you think will help, such as a
  heated blanket, socks, or extra pillows. The hospital staff is
  busy, so they may not offer, but they do care that your
  loved one is comfortable.

- If you and your loved one are getting bored, consider
  using this time to have your loved one tell you about old
  times or relatives. You can take some notes or even record
  on your phone and have some living history documented.
  Oral history is a wonderful gift and capturing some of it as
  you go can take your mind off things.

Be aware, your parent may experience delirium in the hospital, which causes them to be confused and act in ways which are upsetting - pulling out their IV, climbing over the bed rails, not knowing what's going on, etc. Your parent may never have been confused prior to the hospital stay but after being there, appears disoriented. This can be stressful to observe. You can help by orienting them to where they are, what day it is, who you are, etc. Remaining close by to reassure them, day and night, is beneficial. Rest assured that once a person is out of the hospital, typically they return to being oriented and don't have delirium symptoms any more.

## HOW TO CARE FOR YOURSELF

Yes, that's right, you must care for yourself in the ER, too. You may be there for hours.

- Ask staff to estimate how long things will take so you can leave the room for a time. Do not feel guilty about leaving; your loved one is being cared for. Get some fresh air.

DAD NOTES: At the VA, I had a hard time coping. Overstimulated, I think. Nowhere to have a quiet conversation or not see so many people. Went to my car and worked about ninety minutes and felt better. I need to remember this. Later went and parked by the beach to unwind. Being away from hospital helps.

- Give your cell phone number to staff so they can call you when an issue comes up or discharge is imminent.

- Call one relative with an update. Ask if they will phone others for you. Remember, you can call people *later* and update them. Things may change a lot in the next few hours, so if you try to keep everyone updated with the latest, you could make yourself nutty.

- Don't expect to do any office work at the ER; multitasking leads to frustration. It was better for me to leaf through a magazine or read a book when I got bored.

- Eat fruits and vegetables and drink lots of water for your brain health.

I used to get a healthy snack and then walk on the beach when my dad had his chemo at the VA in San Francisco. That time in the fresh air did my head a world of good. When I returned to pick him up, I was refreshed and in a good mood. You can take a respite, too. It's okay—and better for everyone—if you take a break yourself.

As much as you can, document *all* that is going on so you can update your computer file. Dad may go through many tests and hospital stays. It's difficult to keep track of all the medical information. He won't recall it all, and neither will you after a while. Don't be angry or frustrated if you have to review what he has been through repeatedly. If you write it down as you go, you can look back and easily get the facts.

Take the time to confide your own feelings to the most understanding friend of all—your diary. This entry is from one of my dad's ER visits; it was a relief to vent.

*DAD NOTES: I feel alone here, like I have no support system. This is a roller coaster of Dad's being well then crashing. In the ER, no one tells you how long you will be there, you wait for hours, unable to move, get work done. Fragmented day, fluorescent lights, awful!*

For more advice on how to deal with your own stress level, and find some peace, you can jump ahead to Chapter 11.

# CHAPTER 9

# Tips for a Successful Hospital Discharge

You may arrive at the part of the journey when your loved was hospitalized. I empathize. This can be an exhausting time.

The guidelines for taking care of yourself offered in Chapter 11 apply here. So skip ahead if you need to, and really inhale these lifesaving instructions. Be sure to get enough breaks, enough sleep, enough support from loved ones, and enough time to vent.

## DISCHARGE 101

I've found that hospital discharge day is a busy and stressful time. It's very easy for oversights to occur, which can lead to another hospital stay. Take the time to get complete instructions *before* you leave the hospital.

See the end of this chapter for a handy "Hospital Discharge Checklist" you can use. It recaps what is described in this chapter.

The staff member helping with the discharge can go by several names: social worker, discharge planner, case manager, or nurse. For our purposes, we'll use the term "discharge planner" (DP).

Here's what *should* happen: The discharge process begins shortly after your loved one is admitted to the hospital. The DP should ask how things are at home and explain the anticipated discharge plan, subject to change, of course. If a staff member doesn't approach you, approach them about a plan as soon as possible after arrival. They should be willing to hear your thoughts and work to address concerns.

Too many times the family gets a call from the discharge planner saying, "Your dad is going home tomorrow." You panic, especially if you're worried he doesn't have what he needs at home.

CAUTION: a hospital staff member may try to discharge your loved one before there is a thought-out, coordinated, safe plan in place.

You are within your rights to say, "You can't discharge my dad today. It's not safe for him to go home yet."

You may need time to get grab bars or handrails installed. You may need to hire in-home help, or you may need to find an assisted living community that will welcome your parent with open arms. If it is not safe for him to go home yet, speak up! Those assertive words should give you some much-needed time to put into place the care your loved one needs.

# TO CONSIDER BEFORE DISCHARGE DAY

## EQUIPMENT

Discuss needed safety equipment (referred to as durable medical equipment or DME)

- Cane
- Walker
- Wheelchair
- Grab bars
- Commode (portable toilet that can be close to bedside)
- Shower chair (parent can sit in shower if too weak or dizzy to stand)
- Portable oxygen

Ask the DP what equipment might be needed at home, who will order it, if Medicare will cover the cost, and how it will get to where Dad is going.

You may want to buy something called a **portable ramp.**

*(Photo courtesy of Revolutions, Inc.)*

This ramp folds out over the stairs so Dad can get up a slope more easily. Single Fold Ramp from www.Spinlife.com.

If privacy is an issue, consider placing the ramp at the back entrance.

## WHAT IF MEDICARE DOESN'T COVER NEEDED EQUIPMENT?

In my town we have a medical equipment recycling closet.

Many communities have a similar place, run by volunteers, that recycles shower chairs, wheelchairs, lift chair, canes, and even unused boxes of Depends. You can pick up what you need and donate what you don't use. Find out if your community has any type of recycling closet, or look online for used medical equipment.

## TRAINING

Ask about any exercises and treatments to be done at home. Many times I request that the hospital's physical therapist shows the family or hired caregivers how to safely transfer and move the patient. You want all the people involved in Dad's care to know how to care for him, and themselves, safely. Using correct body mechanics is crucial.

Feel free to ask for written directions.

## TRANSPORT

Staff may expect you to drive Dad home, or for him to drive himself, unless told otherwise. However, you are under no obligation to drive him home.

Dad will be weak from the hospital stay, and safety is important for *both* of you. You don't want to hurt yourself or take on more than you can handle, so feel free to say no.

If you don't want to drive him home, ask the discharge planner to make other arrangements. If he needs to go home with a wheelchair, the DP may arrange for nonemergency wheelchair transport. The transport company driver will wheel Dad out of the hospital, drive him home, wheel him off the van, and get him into his home.

A one-way van ride in my area costs about thirty to fifty dollars. It may save your back and your nerves, so if you can afford it, do it.

## DAY OF DISCHARGE

On discharge day, the DP comes to the room to give instructions for going home.

Your parent may be like my clients and my dad. They are so preoccupied with putting on their clothes and gathering things they don't hear the DP's instructions. Try to be there, since he may not be listening closely. You want to prevent errors that could lead to readmission.

*DAD NOTES: I remember my father hollering at the DP. She was going over the home instructions and needed him to sign the release form. He said, "No! I'm not signing anything. I'm going home to die!" It was embarrassing for me—and heartbreaking, too. He wasn't accurate. He lived a long time after that, but at that moment he was hopeless and angry. Your parent may have similar emotions.*

The DP provides *written* discharge instructions. Even if they are not fully digestible now, read them when you have time. You will learn what is expected to be done after the hospital stay to aid your parent's recovery.

## MEDICATION

Ask to see the full list of medications Dad is going home with, and find out what prescriptions need to be filled at the pharmacy. Compare this with the list of medications you made earlier. Is there a new medication? Has a medication been discontinued or a dose changed?

With your parent present, ask a hospital staff member about instructions for any new meds—and any possible side effects. If there's no time to do this, ask the pharmacist.

Pick up medication at the pharmacy *before* you wheel Dad down to the car, since it may be a long wait.

## FOLLOW-UP APPOINTMENTS

Ask about the schedule for follow-up appointments or tests. These are typically listed in the discharge instructions.

You'll also want to know if the hospital discharge plan includes an order from the doctor for home health care. Typically this order is for a nurse, physical, occupational, or speech therapist to conduct therapy at home. These professionals provide visits for a limited time and are covered by Medicare.

If home health care is ordered, ask for the agency phone number, in case you need to follow up and find out when a staff member is coming out. Get a business card for the company, if possible. Add it to the business-card holder sheet in your Communication Binder.

Ask the discharge planner about any signs and symptoms you should be concerned about after discharge. Find out the symptoms that are serious enough to warrant a call to the doctor.

Remember: care managers, like me, can help you through this transition time. We act as patient and family advocates. We are there on discharge day to read the discharge instructions and to try to minimize communication breakdowns during the transition back home. (See Chapter 14.)

## HOSPITAL DISCHARGE CHECKLIST

Use this checklist early and often during your loved one's hospitalization. Skip what doesn't apply.

Discharge Planner:

Date of Admission:

Reason for Admission:

Planned Date for Going Home:

### Equipment and Safety

☐ What equipment will be needed at home? (e.g., a wheelchair, walker, hospital bed, or bedside commode)

☐ Do you have any of this equipment at home in good working order? If so, let DP know.

☐ What equipment company will be used for delivery of medical equipment?

☐ Is oxygen being delivered?

☐ When will equipment be delivered? Give your schedule so you can be there.

☐ Will Medicare cover cost of equipment? If not, will supplemental insurance cover costs? If not, what is the out-of-pocket cost?

What will patient need help with at home?

- ☐ Bathing
- ☐ Dressing
- ☐ Toileting
- ☐ Walking
- ☐ Eating
- ☐ Transferring
- ☐ Transportation
- ☐ Bill paying
- ☐ Medication
- ☐ Climbing stairs
- ☐ Cooking
- ☐ Help at night
- ☐ Wound care
- ☐ Injections

## TRAINING AND AFTERCARE

☐ Arrange for the discharge plan to be explained when the whole family can be present with the patient. Invite any person you are hiring to help at home to hear the plan also.

Family often incorrectly assumes that any care needed at home after a hospital stay will be covered by insurance.

If your loved one needs a skilled professional to do nursing care, physical therapy, speech therapy, or occupational therapy, the doctor can order home health care.

If your loved one doesn't qualify for home health care agency services, you have to pay for any help from a home care company or do it yourself. This is nonmedical help. What a difference one word makes: home health care versus home care.

☐ Ask for any training needed from staff ahead of discharge. This can include safe movement, getting in and out of a car, using an inspirometer, negotiating stairs, and so forth.

☐ When will DP meet with patient and family regarding discharge plans?

☐ Will there be home health care or therapy provided by the hospital/medical plan?

    ☐ If so, when will the first visit happen?

    ☐ Contact info for person visiting:

☐ Will the patient need ongoing home care not covered by insurances?

☐ If so, can discharge planner arrange initial contact with a private-pay nonmedical home care agency? Paperwork can be signed prior to going home.

☐ Name of home care companies and contact info:


☐ What signs and symptoms should you be concerned about if you see them at home? When should you call the doctor or return to the hospital?


## MEDICATION

☐ Ask to see the full list of medications at discharge.

☐ Take a look at the medication list you made at home. How do the lists compare? Is there a new medication? Has a medication been discontinued or a dose changed?

☐ Communicate with DP about the specific pharmacy to fill any prescriptions, unless you will be using the hospital pharmacy.

☐ Pick up prescriptions *before* you get your loved one ready to leave the hospital.

☐ Ask discharge planner about transportation.

    ☐ By ambulance
    ☐ By private transport company
    ☐ By family

☐ Confirm location to be transported:

☐ Confirm transport date and time:

*CHAPTER 10*

# Home From the Hospital

Congratulations! You got your parent out of the hospital. Now what? Well, if they are headed home, that may become a very busy place.

In the hospital, patient activities are scheduled, and there are professionals at all hours. All that changes when Dad returns home. There's a lot for him and the family to manage—often without help.

Typically family caregivers have no training or experience. Most people just figure it out as they go along.

Let's map out how to coordinate this kind of effort.

1) As soon as your parent is safely home, read the hospital discharge instructions. Follow them carefully and call the doctor's office with any questions.

2) Put the discharge instructions in your Communication Binder, along with any other information from this hospital stay, under HOSPITAL PAPERS. Add dates of hospitalization to the top section of your computer file for easy reference.

3) Create an online calendar for others to view. Check out LotsaHelpingHands.com or CaringBridge.org. Here you can post what you need help with: transportation, shopping, errands, laundry, and so forth. People with permission to view the calendar can sign up to do a task or two. That makes your life easier: there are no phone calls to make, and people choose what they feel comfortable doing.

4) Schedule a family meeting or family conference call. If you don't have siblings, are there other family members who might be willing to assist in taking care of your loved one? If so, ask if they might be willing to talk through the tasks that are ahead and offer ways they might contribute.

5) Have family members complete the Support-System Questionnaire in Chapter 7, if they haven't already. This will help inform everyone what professional services need to be paid versus what the family wants to handle.

6) Be realistic during the meeting with your family. Is it reasonable to ask your sister to help manage Dad's finances at this time if she can't manage her own money? Or, if your brother is a big-picture thinker, why ask him to do detail work, like setting up the medications? Honor each other's skills and divvy up responsibilities accordingly.

I suggest you train your parents on what can be expected of you, in terms of caring for them. The sooner you do this, the better.

# REMEDIES FOR KEEPING PARENTS HEALTHY AT HOME

## MOVEMENT

We are not made for staying in bed twenty-two to twenty-four hours a day. Hospitals are notorious for letting people stay in bed way too much. Don't get me started.

While patients are in the hospital, they lose muscle strength. Here's a sobering figure that I tell clients: experts estimate that for each day we are in the hospital, it takes three to seven days to regain our baseline strength. So if Mom is in the hospital for seven days, it will be twenty-one to forty-nine days until she is back to her own version of "normal."

Everyone needs to encourage Mom to get up and move as much as possible, unless doctor's orders say otherwise.

Walk, walk, and walk some more, outside if possible. The added benefits of getting out the door are sunshine more vitamin D for stronger bones and a rise in serotonin for combatting depression. Mom will see, hear, and smell the outside world, which is good for her brain and good for her emotional and psychological health. If you walk with her, you both benefit.

Exercises will help her to breathe deeper, helping to stave off pneumonia. Walking may reduce blood clots. These are good outcomes, so don't take no for an answer. Start small and add distance as she can handle it.

If walking is not an option, consider doing range-of-motion limb exercises daily. Look online for a tutorial that makes sense for your needs to see how to do passive exercises.

DAD NOTES: *When my dad was spending too much time indoors during his cancer treatments, I suggested that he walk or sit in the sun. He jumped on that idea and went outside with the paper daily, actually getting a tan from sitting on the balcony. I'd come up the stairs of his apartment building and find him outside, shirt off, reading happily, and looking content, soaking up some sun. Initially, he was really weak and short of breath and could barely walk outside his apartment. But with time and effort, he prided himself on ambling around the perimeter of his apartment building upstairs. He increased his stamina until he was able to go downstairs and get his mail. He took joy in regaining his strength, and he loved measuring his progress and reporting it to me.*

## FOLLOW-UP APPOINTMENTS

Get a large wall calendar and keep it centrally located in your parent's home where all can see it.

Mark each appointment on the calendar, whether a person is coming to see your mom or if she has an appointment out.

Note who will be driving or accompanying her and list contact information.

When you get an appointment card, transfer the date and the time immediately to the calendar. Seeing commitments reinforces structure to the day.

After you note the appointments on the calendar, put the business card in the plastic sheet in the Communication Binder for future reference.

Mark the calendar each time Mom exercises. This will keep her accountable. Plus, everyone can track her progress and compliment her on her determination and consistency.

Once Mom is home from the hospital, this is an opportune time to offer to accompany her to a doctor's appointment, especially if you have not been able to do so before.

Be sure to arrange transportation to appointments. You may want to call the nonemergency medical transport company that brought your mom home from the hospital. There may be a van service for disabled people that offers transportation. You can meet at her appointment if you will not be driving her.

## MEDICATION MANAGEMENT

Medication errors are very common and can result in ER visits.

Helping your parent stay on top of meds can be a big job, so budget enough time to handle this task.

If you haven't done this already, now is a good time to read Chapter 1 and learn how to use a pill box.

## ENGAGEMENT

We all need a reason to get up each day. What we "have to do" shapes our day and our lives.

When people are stuck at home, they can get cabin fever. Without tasks to accomplish or a reason to get up, depression, boredom, and loneliness can set in.

Encourage your parent to dress in street clothing and do basic grooming every day, to the extent that they can. If needed, try a Sonic Care toothbrush which requires less hand dexterity for keeping teeth and gums healthy.

Consider what your parent enjoys and create a regular "job" around it. We all need to be needed.

Here's what I did to help get my dad out of the house:

I asked him to get my mail at the PO Box.

I asked him to drive me home when I dropped off my car to be repaired. I asked him to come over, set up the poker table, and teach some friends how to play. I also asked his advice for home repairs and borrowed his tools.

When Dad developed an interest in cooking, I asked him to make me dinner, so he could try out his new recipes. We ate together often.

He also played the stock market with my sister. They talked daily about how the market was doing, and he learned to use an iPad and use E-Trade Financial.

And, amazingly, he played online chess with a young friend—all this technical prowess from a man who needed a year to figure out how to use his cell phone. Where there is interest, there is engagement!

## CHORES

Be alert to what day-to-day chores need to be done. Show up consistently to handle the tasks you agreed to handle, so your parent can depend on that, but only help until your parent can resume doing them. It is not healthy to prolong their dependency.

> Check out this phrase: "learned helplessness." Professionals use it to describe what can happen when you do too much for someone, helping beyond what is currently needed. We see this often in institutions. Older people get used to letting us do things for them and then learn to be helpless. Let Mom or Dad do whatever part of a task they can. Back off as they regain their strength and confidence. Remember their need for engagement.

# HOW TO KEEP YOUR CAREGIVING MANAGEABLE

Ask your Mom or Dad to keep a shopping list. Encourage them to go with you to the store. They need to use their energy to sleep better. They need to get out in the world.

To arrive home with energy and sanity, my golden rule is to go with your parent on only *one* errand/outing per day. I know the bank may be near the pharmacy, but going to both in one day is often too much. Just do one task and then head home with Mom. You may be thinking, "What? That's not efficient!" You're right. It pains me to do one thing, too. In the long run, however, I think you will both arrive home less stressed. Go at their pace, not yours.

If they refuse to go out with you, do yourself a favor and schedule shopping only once a week.

DAD NOTES: *I told Dad I'm only shopping Wednesday and Saturday for him. And on Wednesday I called and got his list. He was ready. My daughter and he made fun of me. He said, "Yeah, I guess your mom doesn't want to shop every day." No kidding.*

Often times the *daily* request for an item from the store is code for "I'm lonely." You know Mom is not going to perish if she doesn't have shampoo...but she can make it seem urgent, can't she?

DAD NOTES: *I hate not making money on a workday when spending time at the VA. So I decided to make Dad's appointments in the afternoon so I can at least work in morning, when I'm most productive. Can't get much done on computer in waiting rooms with multiple interruptions. Or I can get my daughter or another to drive him to appointments. Cheaper to pay $28/hour than lose my hourly wage.*

# CHAPTER 11

# Care for Yourself...or Else!

I realize that you're reading this book to help someone else, but I want to add some words about looking out for yourself during this process. If you're thinking of skipping this chapter, don't. Seriously. It's the most important chapter in this book. The adage, "You *must* take care of yourself in order to be of use to others," is critical in elder care land.

---

You may wonder...
How did I even become a caregiver?
How did I become so exhausted?  Will this ever end?

---

Most people don't think about becoming caregivers. They start doing it out of love and/or obligation, and soon it can be all consuming, part of what we do and who we are. It was probably gradual. Here's a little parable to illustrate:

Say you meet a friend about to enter her front door, and she has a big bag of groceries in her arms. She asks you to hold the heavy bag for a minute. What do you say? You say, "Sure thing," and you wait while she digs out her keys. You follow her inside and set the groceries down.

But what if your friend took a year to find her keys and just left you standing there with the bag? Would you agree to that? Could you agree to that?

My point is that caregiving begins with agreeing to hold the bag for a minute. Then it becomes this heavy thing you carry around. You have no idea how to put it down or how to take some groceries out to lighten the bag.

## SIX SIGNS OF CAREGIVER FATIGUE AND BURNOUT AND SIX REMEDIES

### SIGN #1

You want to run away and escape from everything! I sure did. You are feeling crushed between handling both your own life and your parent's. Your alcohol intake may have increased; this is important to notice.

Caution: If you're abusing a substance, this may be part of burnout, too. You need to address your use of alcohol, drugs, or painkillers. Talk to a professional counselor to evaluate how your behavior is linked to caregiving and how to turn the pressure off.

REMEDY: Go somewhere—the park, the movies, the mall, the gym. These activities are self-renewing, and act as an immediate balm. I had to tell myself: put away the to-do list. Don't do one more errand. Stop, go play, recharge. You have permission, too.

## SIGN #2

You notice your routine is off or you keep getting sick. I could see my car needed servicing. I was eating unhealthy food late at night, and my exercise routine decreased. I gained 17 pounds in two years. These were all signs I was approaching caregiver burnout.

**REMEDY:** Book the oil change, doctor appointment, or nail appointment, mute your phone, or make a healthy meal. Get your own life in order. For each errand you run for your parent, do one for yourself. Keep the scales balanced. Remember, your life is important, too!

## SIGN #3

You begin to feel animosity toward your parent. You say or do something mean, uncharacteristic, or unkind to the person you are caring for. Sometimes verbal and physical abuse occurs.

**DAD NOTES:** *I got mad one afternoon when my dad questioned the brand of an over-the-counter medication I bought for him, which he asked for...It was the end of a long day and I lost it. I just threw down some paperwork I brought over, left the medication on the table, and angrily walked out. I didn't need this crap. Enough is enough. I was not feeling appreciated, and it was the last straw.*

**REMEDY:** Do less. Get off the merry-go-round. Do something that restores you to your more balanced self. It may be time to attend a support group or individual therapy to cope with caregiver burden.

SIGN #4

You avoid socializing.

REMEDY: Reluctance to go out with friends might mean you're nesting and rebuilding. That can be a good thing but it's also important to hang out with your friends. Take the first step and give a friend a call. It really can ease caregiving stress.

DAD NOTES: *I feel as though each evening something goes wrong with Dad. I went home Wednesday night and just watched So You Think You Can Dance on TV and talked with my housemate. He noticed I was sad and heavy at first but better as the night wore on. I think just having a normal routine for a few hours, like I used to—my own rather than Dad's—was healthy. Need to tell people how important getting back in touch with normalness is to their being able to cope.*

SIGN #5

This is dark, I know, but you may secretly hope your loved one dies or moves away, and you really don't care where. You may want to drop Mom off at your brother's house and keep driving into the sunset. Contemplating the death of your parent is completely normal. I hear this regularly from clients, and I felt this despair myself. When my dad would go away, I sometimes wondered if he never returned, how would I feel? When I was overwhelmed, I figured this was good—less work for me. Other times I would cry, thinking how awful that I'm even thinking that I hoped he never came back.

This is part of caregiver burnout. You are now doing too much caring and worrying. This also may mean you lack proper caregiver support.

**REMEDY:** *You have to get help.* When someone asks what they can do to help, be prepared with an answer. Maybe they can do the shopping or drive Mom to an event. Maybe you can ask them to do a chore *you* need done for you, while you tend to Mom.

This also signals that you need to take time off in some way—a vacation, a stay-cation, or even asking someone to step in so you don't need to see Dad for a while. My sister came into the picture big-time when I got angry with my father and walked out of his apartment. Thanks, Sis.

Friends usually want to help but aren't sure how. And, ya gotta ask! Make a list of tasks you do. Ask yourself who could do one or two of them to lighten your load.

I have this offbeat idea: What if we switched parents and you took my mom to lunch and I took yours? I believe it would be good for all four of us. We hear someone's stories for the first time, get a new perspective from them if we are sharing our lives and struggles, and develop an appreciation for them. It also builds in a natural backup for each of us, without any officialness.

## SIGN #6

The phone rings. You see it's your loved one, and you roll your eyes. *"What now?"* I can relate. You don't answer, but then you feel guilty. You worry that it might be an emergency, and you've let

Dad down. At the same time, you know that if you pick up that phone, you're going to explode.

DAD NOTES: *One time Dad called me from the emergency room and asked me to bring him some cough drops at five o'clock on a Saturday morning! I told him, "No, sorry; ask a nurse,"* and I went back to sleep.

REMEDY: Let the call go to voicemail, and check the message when you're in a better frame of mind; most likely, the information can wait. If it's a true emergency, Dad can push the button on the personal emergency response system or call 911.

Sometimes it's all a matter of perspective.

DAD NOTES: *One day after Dad's radiation treatment, I was driving him back home. He was frail and complaining. His cell phone rang, and suddenly his demeanor changed. He was positive and upbeat. I felt I was driving with Dr. Jekyll and Mr. Hyde.*

*I thought, Oh, I see. You're all sunshine and light with your buddy while I'm stuck with all the work and complaining. Grumble, grumble.*

*Upon reflection, it was a good thing listening to the way he related his condition to another. He wanted others to believe he was doing well.*

*I realize, too, that he could be himself with me. He didn't need to pretend things were easy if they were not. I consider it a gift that I got to hear his authentic feelings.*

When do we learn to take care of ourselves?

Is it when we reach a certain age?
Is it modeled for us?
Is it after a diagnosis of disease?
Is it never?
When will you start to take care of yourself if you are not doing that now?
Why will you begin?
How can you do it?

One doctor I heard about wrote prescriptions to caregivers, such as, "Don't visit your parent this weekend." Or, "Take one-week vacation." This empowered the caregivers since it was doctor's orders and official. You should not expect yourself to work seven days a week and not take a break, no other "jobs" require that.

Parents may not see all you are doing, and they may not appreciate that you're doing so much. They may not know the impact their care is having on you. They are looking at life from a changed perspective, and it may be a slightly selfish one at this point, or they may be unaware due to memory loss. When they're ailing, they're not in the best shape to parent you, which you still secretly may want.

You have to give yourself permission to take breaks for play and relaxation. When you take a few days off, you'll feel better, and your parent may appreciate you even more when you return.

I witness the strain of caregiving on client families daily. It can take a toll on health and lifespan. Please reduce your load so you can remain healthy. I have had caregivers get terminally ill and die and their parents go on living for years.

DAD NOTES: *I went to a business meeting after my father died, one I normally attended but had not been to for several months. People came over and said I looked great...new haircut and lipstick. One woman asked if I had been on vacation. Interesting. My dad died, and I began to attend to my own needs again, so my face relaxed. I was no longer taking care of two lives.*

Self-renewal doesn't have to cost anything nor take a lot of time.

## ACTIVITIES JUST FOR YOU

Do something you love doing. Rediscover what inspires and recharges you with positive energy. Maybe something you haven't done for a long time:

- Paint/draw or color
- Hike
- Watch uninterrupted TV
- Play with your pet
- Garden
- Visit a friend
- Go to the library
- Listen to music
- Lie in the grass or on the beach
- Window shop
- Go to a park and watch little kids
- Read
- Take a nap
- Stretch
- Dance
- Call a friend, or make a date to meet
- Swim
- Play a board game or cards

# CHAPTER 12

# When Mom Says "No Way" to Paid Help

Mom is home. You've been helping a lot while she recovers, but now what? Well, you can continue helping *forever*. Seriously, some make this choice without realizing or acknowledging it.

You probably can't and shouldn't keep living her life *and* yours forever.

You may be interested in hiring some help. You have to put your foot down, gently and compassionately—much easier said than done.

Let's imagine you've already tried having the conversation with Mom about getting some assistance, and it didn't go well. Right? I didn't just read your mind. It's rare for a loved one to agree to hired help, for obvious and not so obvious reasons.

*Before* bringing up the subject again, close your eyes and imagine that **you** are the one needing help. Change places with your loved one for a minute.

How would you want others to approach you if you were no longer able to care for yourself independently?

How would you want someone to talk with you about paying for help?

We adults don't want to need help nor do we want to admit we need it. Getting in touch with how it would be for you, can help shape the conversation with your parent.

Your parent may have said any of the following things when you brought up the subject of paid help:

I don't need help (not true)
I can't afford help (may not be true)
I don't want a stranger in my house (who would?)

## ARGUMENT 1—I DON'T NEED HELP!

Think about this. Does she have a point? After all, *you* are helping and that may be sufficient. If you keep taking her to appointments, doing her laundry, refilling her medications, she will let you. Rarely have I heard a parent say, "Hey, Honey, you don't need to do this. I'll pay for help." You're laughing because you know I'm right. She has no reason to tell you *not* to do so much.

But really, this can be a tender subject. It may be painful for your mom to admit she needs help. If you do the work, it can seem casual, as if you just love stopping by and doing things, and you may. For me, I got overwhelmed and missed my life.

Maintaining her health and lifestyle can seem like a much more serious problem if she has to pay a stranger. I'm all for doing what you can to help. I did so for my dad. But when it goes on for years or morphs into helping a person shower, use the toilet, and so forth, it may be uncomfortable or even impossible.

> Having paid home care employees is usually better than family help in the long run because it allows you to keep your normal role as son, daughter, spouse, or friend.

Here's a comparison your folks may understand. Most likely, they have paid for the professional services of a doctor, lawyer, dentist, and/or accountant over the years and not depended on you for these services. Couch the home help as another professional service.

If Mom is still resistant, stress that the help is for a specific chore or set amount of time. For example: Mom, I know you prefer that I help you, but this month I can't, sorry. We are going to use a home care professional for one month because:

- I need a break.
- I'm scheduled for surgery.
- I'm running away to join the circus.
- Work is busy.
- The kids are heading back to school.

## ARGUMENT 2—I CAN'T AFFORD HELP!

Money. The big pushback. Sometimes it's true that funds are limited and paid home care will be unrealistic. More often, though, there are funds, but Dad won't use them. Period. Consider, too, that Dad's changes may have been gradual, and he may think he's coping well. However, if he is declining, the question becomes: Can he afford the consequences of *not* having help?

Some consequences can be life threatening:

- Various illnesses arise from being unclean due to lack of regular hygiene
- Food poisoning after eating bad food
- Medication errors, diabetic episodes
- Poor nutrition from not cooking or lacking fresh food

Other less risky consequences may be a smelly house because the garbage is not taken out, a filthy bathroom, and dirty dishes in the sink.

If finances are limited or a person has the assets but refuses to use them on home care, you have a couple of options.

You can pay for the home care yourself, as a gift. Or you can pay for the help, knowing you may receive assets (as reimbursement) from the estate in the future.

If no one in the family can afford private home care, states may have a program to help. Go to www.Eldercare.gov to learn what's available in your state.

Another solution to the argument of not wanting to pay for a home care helper can be that *you* get paid to help. It's not unreasonable to be paid for your continued help, especially if this means you are sacrificing your day job. Your services have value!

> Stop and ask yourself: How much do I want to do or continue to do? Would I feel better if I were paid to do this and if so, what compensation feels right? Tell your parent you will continue to help but your time is worth $\_\_ dollars per hour. Ask, "Would you be comfortable paying me that rate?"

DAD NOTES: *I had a home care agency meet with my dad. During the visit, he learned that what I had been doing for nothing would cost $28.50 per hour. He signed on but never called them. When I pushed him to use the company, after scrubbing his bathroom on my hands and knees, he said, "I'll pay you forty dollars an hour." I made forty dollars for that hour. He passed away before we could call the home care company after that.*

## ARGUMENT 3—I DON'T WANT A STRANGER IN MY HOUSE!

Who does? Not me, and not you. Anyone is a stranger on the first visit. Even Mom's husband was a stranger when they met.

To soothe this concern, I recommend that you or another trusted person are present the first time the person from the home care company comes to the home. You can help explain what is needed, and then help orient the caregiver. Most likely your mom will feel comfortable after that.

Regardless of what topic you need to address with Mom or Dad, approach it in a loving way, but set your mind on a successful outcome. Don't be sheepish or casual when presenting the idea of paid care. If your parent senses you are not serious, they will rebuff the idea. If you need, tell them you will reduce how often you visit until they get paid help.

## E-MAILS WITH MY FRIENDS FROM 11/9/2014:

*On 11/9/14 5:23 p.m., Kira Reginato <kira@lifegcm.com> wrote:*

*Hi gals,*

*Got dad picked up from hospital today, on new heart medication but should be okay...I guess. I will be calling a home care agency to visit him and get registered so I can have back up. Whether he likes it or not! I was beyond the beyond this week with 5 days of caring.    Kira*

**Their responses:**

*Thanks for the update, Kir. I am so glad Dad is home for now. It is such an intense roller coaster time, and exhausting to the max as you being the point and only person. Woowee.    Rebecca*

*Glad you are setting things up to support Dad and yourself. That's what you taught me to do :) Love to both of you.    Cheryl*

# CHAPTER 13

# Getting Started with Paid Help

You have two choices when you don't want or can't assist your parent:

Hire someone privately.

Hire an employee through a home care company.

Note: This is not a home *health* care company. That extra word "health" means that medical services are provided and Medicare covers them. This is doctor ordered. What you want is day-to-day nonmedical assistance.

## OPTION #1—PRIVATE HIRES

Hiring someone privately as your household employee can be done, but I don't recommend it, and here's why. You will have many responsibilities, such as interviewing candidates, running background checks, handling payroll, getting workers' compensation insurance, reprimanding the person, filling in when the person doesn't show, and training when Mom has new needs. And if the privately hired person can't make the shift, moves, or quits, you will need to start over.

That's a lot and can be exhausting. You are looking to *lighten* your load.

PITFALLS OF A PRIVATE HIRE: One adult daughter whose father had dementia told me about Lisa, a private caregiver who was doing a good job but had back pain and stopped coming. "I will never rely so heavily on one person again. My dad got used to Lisa coming, and while she was out, he went backward and declined. Even though we got someone to fill in, we were too long without help in between. When Lisa returned to work, Dad didn't interact with her in the same way. He refused to go out of the house with her anymore."

To learn more about hiring a caregiver privately vs. using an agency, see Compare Your Choices and Find the Right Caregiver charts on next pages.

# Compare Your Choices

## Full Service Agencies
The Agency is the Employer.
These agencies typically screen, train and employ home care aides.
Agencies supervise caregivers and may provide back-up caregiving
services if the primary caregiver is ill or can not provide care. They
withhold taxes and contribute to workers' compensation and unem-
ployment insurance. Agencies typically carry liability insurance and
do criminal background checks.

## Referral Agencies
The Consumer is the Employer.
These agencies place caregivers with consumers and generally
collect a placement fee. Some referral agencies charge an hourly
rate that includes both the agency fee and the aide's wage. The
referral agency typically does not pay employer/employee payroll
taxes or workers' compensation insurance. The consumer must
assume all of the responsibilities of an employer, including the
withholding and payment of taxes, and worker's compensation
insurance, as required by law.

## Hiring Privately
The Consumer is the Employer.
Independent providers of care, such as aides or companions, can be
hired privately by the consumer. Once an employer/employee relationship is established, the consumer must assume all of the responsibilities of an employer, including the withholding and payment of taxes,
and worker's compensation insurance, as required by law.

**\*\*Chart Key**  ✓ = included   **?**  = may not be included

# Find The Right Caregiver

| | Full Service Agency | Referral Agency | Private Hire |
|---|---|---|---|
| Locate, screen, interview, train | ✓ | ? | Consumer Responsibility |
| Check employer references | ✓ | ? | Consumer Responsibility |
| Verify USA work authorization | ✓ | ? | Consumer Responsibility |
| Withhold payroll taxes | ✓ | ? | Consumer Responsibility |
| Negotiate salary/benefits | ✓ | ? | Consumer Responsibility |
| Determine work schedule, cover days off and holidays | ✓ | Consumer Responsibility | Consumer Responsibility |
| **SUPERVISION** | | | |
| Professional on-site supervision | ✓ | Consumer Responsibility | Consumer Responsibility |
| Caregiver replacement, if necessary | ✓ | ? | Consumer Responsibility |
| **LIABILITY** | | | |
| Workers' compensation insurance | ✓ | Consumer Responsibility | Consumer Responsibility |
| Payroll requirements (Social Security, Medicare and other taxes.) | ✓ | Consumer Responsibility | Consumer Responsibility |
| Professional liability insurance for caregiver | ✓ | ? | Consumer Responsibility |

(Charts provided by HCAOA.org)

# OPTION #2—USE A HOME CARE COMPANY

There are many home care companies to choose from that provide nonmedical help. You can choose from companionship and personal care services:

Monitor diet and eating
Help with morning and nighttime care
Help arrange appointments
Assist with walking and getting in and out of bed
Prepare grocery lists and shop
Reminisce
Alzheimer's care
Provide medication reminders
Provide transportation
Do light housekeeping
Help to toilet
Pick up prescriptions
Do laundry
Change linens
Help with bathing and dressing
Plan, prepare and clean up meals
Make bed
Play games, discuss current events

Ask friends for recommendations. Look online under "Home Care" in your area.

In 2016, new laws went into effect for California home care companies, requiring them to be licensed. Many other states have been licensing their home care companies for years.

## SCREENING AGENCIES

1) Call a couple of agencies to see how responsive they are in the first exchange. Go with the one that seems best to you. Ask if they are licensed. If so, you know they are meeting the state requirements.

2) Be candid when the home care company asks about your mom's preferences in a care companion. Does your mom prefer a female or male caregiver? Does she believe she needs a tall person to help transfer from a chair to her bed?

3) Once you provide information about your mom to the agency, they will schedule a time to meet her to review services they offer and their pricing. They will learn about her particular needs and then ask your mom to sign their service contract.

4) It's that easy. Mom can now begin with a caregiver. The agency sends someone whom they think matches what she needs. However, if Mom prefers, they can send potential caregivers to meet her, so she can choose who she wants. Some companies I have worked with charge for this interview time, and some don't.

# FIRST DAYS USING HOME CARE AGENCY

NOTE: If your parent has some memory loss or confusion, you might want to be present with the caregiver at first, telling your mom that the person is a friend of yours. If the two get along, then on the next visit your "friend" can take your parent grocery shopping or to lunch. The benefits for you are obvious.

Be sure to have more than one employee meet and work a few shifts for Mom, if possible. This way she has an alternate helper. The primary caregiver your mom likes and depends on may get sick, need a vacation, or leave. The industry has a lot of turnover, unfortunately.

1) Have the employee make the initial visit with the intent of building rapport with your parent. On the second or third visit, they can begin doing tasks.

2) Begin with chores that don't involve personal care, if feasible. Simple tasks like washing dishes, taking out the garbage, or preparing a snack are good places to start.

Consider your dad's perspective and pace. It's unlikely you would want to run an errand with a stranger you just met, or have them help dress you. Do what Dad would be comfortable with.

3) The home care company typically provides a binder with instructions for the staff and forms for employees to document what they do on their shifts. Feel free to review this binder, and what the employees say, so you have a sense of how things are

going. This is not just for employees. You can add a note, so caregivers coming on shift can read it.

4) Consider creating a do and don't list so all caregivers coming into the house know the rules. If your dad wants to make his own bed, write, "Please don't make bed. Dad does this by himself."

5) I like to provide a personal history fact sheet about the person for employees. It helps the caregivers learn a little bit about whom they are caring for, so that they will be able to engage with your parent in specific, meaningful ways.

On the next page is a wonderful example of what one client family created for caregivers to read about their mom, who has since passed away. If you read this, wouldn't you know how to interact in a more meaningful way?

Thanks to Mrs. Louvar's family for graciously allowing me to share so others may benefit.

Theresa Louvar - November 26, 1921
Born in Brooklyn, NY

Attended beauty school after high school

Married 40 years to _____ deceased 1982

Married 11 years to_____ deceased 1999

3 children _____ and daughter in law_____

5 grandchildren

4 great-grandchildren

Very proud about being a businesswoman

Don't talk about money with her, makes her anxious

Concerned about the cost of living at assisted living home

Reply with, "It costs the same as where you just moved from."

Loves to paint on canvas, do ceramics

Loves the Travel Channel

Has an elephant collection

Likes to go out to dine with her family

Escort to meals

Needs supervision on outings

Likes to hold hands

Has a friend named ___ from ____ who will visit her

Is very social and likes to hear people's life stories

Gets her hair done once a week

Gets a manicure every week

Gets a pedicure once a month

Uses Oil of Olay facial wipes to clean her face daily

Can become agitated and strike out

Usually sleeps well at night

Will need supervision going to bathroom at night to prevent falls

6) Be Prepared: Your dad may fire the caregiver, and you may feel defeated. I tell people that it may take several tries to find the right person(s) to care for your dad. Don't give up just because one experience didn't work.

You get better at interviewing and knowing what will work. Stick with it and don't let Dad push away other caregivers without giving them a try. Parents are sometimes looking for a reason to make the situation not work because they want *you*. It's normal. Hold your ground.

7) It's important to keep in regular touch with the home care company. There will be changes over time, and you will want to supervise them. You should periodically check and modify the list of responsibilities; call the company so it can inform staff.

8) If for any reason the caregiver is not performing as you think they should, feel free to discuss concerns with the home care supervisor or ask for a different employee. Communication is your friend. Don't suffer through! You are paying for this service and it should meet your needs.

If the company is unable to find reliable, competent staff, call another one.

# Using a Geriatric Care Manager

My profession's title is geriatric care manager but it goes by other names, too, such as aging care manager, elder care manager or now even aging life care professional.

In my career, I've used the title geriatric care manager, but nowadays, I call myself an elder care manager or elder care consultant because people understand that more easily. For our purposes, let's just go with "Care Manager" and keep it simple.

## REASONS YOU MIGHT NEED A CARE MANAGER

- You do not have the time to commit to parent care. Guidance is welcome from an expert about how things are likely to unfold in the months or years ahead as well as how to address the issues at hand.

- You have a difficult relationship with your parent. Caring for your parent is extremely hard even if you have a great relationship. It can be intolerable if you have a poor one. In some cases, however, poor relationships have actually improved through the caregiving experience. There is much to consider.

- You're an only child, and it's too much on your shoulders alone.

- You feel powerless. Maybe because it's hard to communicate or collaborate with your parent on their care.

- Your parent has a mental illness or personality disorder, even if not yet diagnosed. Add that to a broken hip or dementia symptoms, and it's a recipe for high stress, chaos, and fear or helplessness for everyone involved.

- You feel more secure getting professional guidance and objectivity.

- It's difficult dividing caregiving tasks among siblings or other family members.

I often see a son-in-law or daughter-in-law get along with the parent better than the adult child. This makes sense because they don't have the history to deal with. A client said her nephew is the "Grandma Whisperer." He can handle Grandma just the right way. Use this to your advantage. I know how frustrating it is to see Dad agree to something your spouse suggests when he refused the same thing with you. But who cares? Let family members help; it's actually very wise and strategic.

## A WORD TO THE ONLY CHILD

The good news is that you get to make all the decisions without arguing with siblings.

The bad news is you get to make all the decisions.

Oh…and be the only one going to appointments, managing finances, and going to the hospital to be medical advocate, fact checker, and comfort monitor, as well as head cheerleader, etc.

## AVOID BEING AN OSTRICH

Honestly, this elder care stuff is difficult, and many of us want to delay doing difficult things. Families often come to us at crisis time.

Not taking care of business, not having a plan for action, typically leads to bad decisions, which may compound into worse outcomes.

That's why I recommend having at least one meeting with a care manager. Some people find a consult helpful when they are just taking on the role of caregiver. Others call us when they find themselves stuck or overwhelmed. You may appreciate a person to turn to for help in this painful, complicated, emotional time.

Having a care manager means that you have a partner on your journey. You don't have to figure out what to do on your own or to reinvent the wheel.

Talking about the issues with a professional can be so helpful and save hours of effort down the line.

# WHAT IS A CARE MANAGER'S SCOPE OF PRACTICE?

- Conduct a professional assessment of your loved one's condition and concerns. I think of us as a one-stop shop of solutions.

- Listen to concerns and suggestions from spouses and adult children. We need to listen before we start solving problems.

- Create a care plan with suggested action steps and resources. Talk with your family about next best steps. This guides decision-making by separating the factual from the emotional.

- I always ask my older clients what their goals are, no matter what their health or cognitive or mental status, and no matter what their family might have in mind for them. This can help shape the care plan in a poignant way.

## CARE MANAGEMENT SERVICES

- Schedule appointments and transportation.
- Contact and consult doctors and other health professionals.
- Arrange and monitor home care agency employees.
- Handle the discharge from the hospital.

- Accompany your parent to appointments as the advocate and note taker, and then follow up once your parent arrives back home.
- Coordinate moves from home to a facility.
- Supervise privately hired caregivers.
- Encourage completion of legal forms.
- Arrange individual, couple, or family therapy. Some care managers are licensed to provide this in addition to care management services.

## CARE MANAGERS DO NOT

- Diagnose physical or mental illness
- Prescribe or administer medications
- Direct medical or nursing care
- Provide physical, occupational or speech therapy

## WHO ARE CLIENTS?

Anyone can hire a care manager: an adult child, the parent, a spouse, a grandchild. We can help long-term or provide a one-time consultation.

I've been asked, "Can I hire you even if my mom and brother don't want your help? Every time I talk to you I feel calm and I get direction." I said "Certainly. We can always help individual members of the family, providing guidance and support."

# KEY QUESTIONS TO ASK WHEN INTERVIEWING A CARE MANAGER

1) What are your credentials, degrees, or certification? Consider a professional with education in gerontology (study of aging), social work, or nursing.

Note: A professional can choose to attain certain certifications; however, no nationally standardized license or certification for geriatric care managers is is *required* at this time.

2) How long have you been doing care management? The more experience, the better. Call at least two firms, if available in your area, to compare.

3) How quickly does the care manager return your call? Pick the one you can see meeting your parent and working well with your family circumstances.

4) Fees? In my area of Northern California, care managers charge $100–$185 per hour, plus travel and mileage in many cases.

5) Can you provide references, testimonials? Check the references.

You may call a care manager one thing, and end up getting the most valuable help in a different area. One family asked me to help their mom, who had dementia. After the first meeting, the daughter wrote, "So far I am impressed with your work. I hope we can get Mom under control." In the end, I didn't get their mom "under control" because her disease was steadily progressing. But I was able to help the family relocate Mom to a more appropriate assisted living facility, which gave her the care and supervision she needed.

Care managers try to be neutral and not judge the way your family operates. We understand that family dynamics are entrenched and complicated, and that issues can't be solved overnight. We use discretion and acumen to gently push forward or advise letting issues go when discussions won't produce results.

Care managers have a complex job, but as creative problem solvers, we enjoy moving families forward in a positive way.

Here's an email from a family member: *"Thank you! You really are so professional and have a nice light, positive air of clarity. You are just what I was hoping for to help us move through this scary time of care giving options. I had been meeting a lot of resistance to moving forward, but know I feel I can relax and know we are going to move forward."*

Visit www.AgingLifeCare.org or www.Longtermcarelink.net to find a care manager in your area.

# FINAL THOUGHTS

I'm working on two other short books. One will have tips on
senior housing options, dementia, and driving concerns. The
other will address sorting out legal and financial issues, as well as
coping with end-of-life issues.

Thank you for reading my book. I hope it provided helpful advice
that makes caregiving more manageable. Please take care of
yourself in the process. I hope, too, that you recognize and
appreciate the smiles, the hugs, and the love that you help nurture.
In my eyes you are a quiet hero.

Closing notes on Dad: *I asked my dad, who lived alone, to move closer
to me as he aged. I'm grateful he agreed. I suggest this to clients all the
time because being nearby makes caregiving so much easier.*

*He said he loved the place he moved to in my small town, and I was glad
I didn't need to drive to San Francisco to see him and care for him at a
distance. Thanks, Dad, for doing that.*

*Before the last two intense months of his cancer treatments, there were
lots of Chinese lunches we shared and yummy dinners, Willits trips and
poker games, walks on the beach, and hugs and kisses. He was my go-to
pal a lot of times.*

*I thought he was doing me a favor by moving close by, but I found out
that, in the end, our caring was mutual. I got to have my dad a few
minutes away as an adult, which brought a new dimension to our relationship. The connection we developed from that ease of seeing each other
is a treasured time we spent, and I got more than I ever thought possible
during the last six years of his life.*

# RESOURCES

For a complete list of resources, visit
www.CallKira.com/Resources

## BOOKS

1. *Stages of Senior Care: Your Step-by-Step Guide to Making the Best Decisions*; Paul and Lori Hogan. McGraw-Hill, 2010
2. *MY MOTHER, YOUR MOTHER: Embracing "Slow Medicine," The Compassionate Approach to Caring for Your Aging Loved Ones*; Dr. Dennis McCullough. HarperCollins, 2008
3. *The Family Guide to Aging Parents*; Carolyn Rosenblatt. 2015
4. *The Patient's Checklist: 10 Simple Hospital Checklists to Keep You Safe, Sane and Organized*; Elizabeth Bailey. Sterling Publishing, 2011
5. *Mom Loves You Best: Forgiving and Forging Sibling Relationships*; Cathy Cress and Kali Cress Peterson. New Horizon Press, 2010
6. *The Emotional Survival Guide for Caregivers: Looking After Yourself and Your Family While Helping an Aging Parent*; Barry Jacobs, PsyD. The Guilford Press, 2006
7. *How to Care for Aging Parents*; Virginia Morris. Workman Publishing, 2014
8. *The Caregiving Zone*; Peggy Flynn. iUniverse, Inc., 2006
9. *Caring is Not Enough – My Last Wishes and Personal Records*; Terry Ann Black, RN. www.caringisnotenough.net, 2012

## MOVIES

*Trouble With the Curve*—Is Clint Eastwood like your Dad? This movie is for you!

*Savages*—Siblings have to care for a father they never liked.

*Two Weeks*—Mom is terminal; adult children come to be with her. Humorous and easy to relate to.

## WEBSITES

Radio podcasts and resources: www.CallKira.com

Information on Adverse Drug Reactions from
The Centers for Disease Control and Prevention:
www.cdc.gov/MedicationSafety/Adult_AdverseDrugEvents.html

Falls Prevention Facts from National Council on Aging:
www.ncoa.org/news/resources-for-reporters/get-the-facts/falls-prevention-facts/

Learn Not to Fall: How Often Falls Occur:
www.learnnottofall.com/content/fall-facts/how-often.jsp

Family Caregiving Facts:
www.cdc.gov/aging/caregiving/facts.htm

MetLife Study of Caregiving Costs to Working Caregivers:
www.metlife.com/mmi/research/caregiving-cost-working-caregivers.html#key findings

Strength for Caregiving:  Tips from Johnson & Johnson and
AARP
www.strengthforcaring.com

Caring From a Distance
www.cfad.org

Caring Today: Support for Caregivers
www.caringtoday.com

Genwich Life Services, LLC Help for the Sandwich Generation
www.genwich.com

Caregivers in Decline: A Close-up Look at the Health Risks of
Caring for a Loved One, 2006
www.caregiving.org/data/Caregivers%20in%20Decline%20Study-
FINAL-lowres.pdf

In California, your parent may qualify for In-Home Supportive
Services (IHSS).  Department of Social Services:
http://www.cdss.ca.gov/agedblinddisabled/PG1785.htm.

# ABOUT THE AUTHOR

Kira Reginato is a gerontologist, elder care manager, and

consultant who knew she enjoyed and wanted to work with older adults since she was in middle school. She ended up making a career of it, with more than 30 years of professional experience.

After caring for elders in medical and community settings, she opened her own elder care management firm, Living Ideas for Elders, in 2007. In 2010, she was awarded a Chamber of Commerce Recognition Award in Petaluma, California, for excellence in service of seniors.

She works everyday helping people navigate the often complex and confusing elder care maze. For two years she faced the challenge on a very personal level when her father's health began to decline and she stepped in as his caregiver. She had a whole new perspective of what her clients were going through, and that made her better at her job. She applied her knowledge and skills to her own situation which made caring for her father easier.

For five years, Reginato hosted two weekly radio shows, *The Elder Care Show* and *Call Kira About Aging*! Podcasts of these shows can be found at CallKira.com.

Reginato is a popular speaker, known for addressing the highs and lows of caregiving with honesty and humor. She knows that taking care of our aging parents can be heart-wrenching and maddening. At the same time, it can be a beautiful, soulful journey.

## Contact Kira Reginato

**P.O. Box 750393, Petaluma CA 94975-0393**

**Phone:** (707) 762-5433

**Email:** Kira@callkira.com

**Website:** CallKira.com

**Linkedin:** CallKiraAboutAging

**Facebook:** CallKiraAboutAging

To order a copy of this book for a relative or friend, visit www.CallKira.com.

Made in the USA
San Bernardino, CA
13 July 2018